Cross Stitch for
SPECIAL OCCASIONS

Dorothea Hall

MEREHURST

Published 1992 by Merehurst Limited
Ferry House, 51-57 Lacy Road, Putney, London SW15 1PR
© Copyright 1992 Merehurst Limited
ISBN 1 85391 166 6
Reprinted 1994

A catalogue record for this book is available from the British Library.

Edited by Diana Brinton
Designed by Maggie Aldred
Photography by Di Lewis
Illustrations by John Hutchinson
Typesetting by BMD Graphics, Hemel Hempstead
Colour separation by Fotographics Limited, UK – Hong Kong
Printed in Hong Kong by Wing King Tong

*Merehurst is the leading publisher of craft books and has an excellent range
of titles to suit all levels. Please send to the address above for our
free catalogue, stating the title of this book.*

SUPPLIERS

The following mail order
company has supplied
frames, trays, cards, etc.,
for making up some of
the projects in this book:

Framecraft Miniatures Limited
148-150 High Street
Aston
Birmingham, B6 4US
England
Telephone (021) 359 4442

*Addresses for Framecraft
worldwide*
Ireland Needlecraft Pty. Ltd.
2-4 Keppel Drive
Hallam, Victoria 3803
Australia

Danish Art Needlework
PO Box 442, Lethbridge
Alberta T1J 3Z1
Canada

Sanyei Imports
PO Box 5, Hashima Shi
Gifu 501-62
Japan

The Embroidery Shop
286 Queen Street
Masterton
New Zealand

Anne Brinkley Designs Inc.
246 Walnut Street
Newton
Mass. 02160
USA

S A Threads and Cottons Ltd.
43 Somerset Road
Cape Town
South Africa

For information on your
nearest stockist of
embroidery cotton,
contact the following:

DMC

UK
DMC Creative World Limited
62 Pullman Road
Wigston
Leicester, LE8 2DY
Telephone: 0533 811040

USA
The DMC Corporation
Port Kearney Bld.
10 South Kearney
N.J. 07032-0650
Telephone: 201 589 0606

AUSTRALIA
DMC Needlecraft Pty
P.O. Box 317
Earlswood 2206
NSW 2204
Telephone: 02599 3088

COATS AND ANCHOR

UK
Kilncraigs Mill
Alloa
Clackmannanshire
Scotland, FK10 1EG
Telephone: 0259 723431

USA
Coats & Clark
P.O. Box 27067
Dept CO1
Greenville
SC 29616
Telephone: 803 234 0103

AUSTRALIA
Coats Patons Crafts
Thistle Street
Launceston
Tasmania 7250
Telephone: 00344 4222

MADEIRA

UK
Madeira Threads (UK) Limited
Thirsk Industrial Park
York Road, Thirsk
N. Yorkshire, YO7 3BX
Telephone: 0845 524880

U.S.A.
Madeira Marketing Limited
600 East 9th Street
Michigan City
IN 46360
Telephone: 219 873 1000

AUSTRALIA
Penguin Threads Pty Limited
25-27 Izett Street
Prahran
Victoria 3181
Telephone: 03529 4400

CONTENTS

$\mathcal{I}$NTRODUCTION

$\mathbf{C}$ross stitch embroidery offers an extraordinarily wide range of decorative effects, of which this book contains a good number of examples. These include simple geometric borders such as those on the Ringbearer's Cushion (Wedding-day Treasures), stylized designs using a single colour as shown in the Traditional Sampler, and more realistic illustrations, such as Randolph Caldecott's 'A Frog he Would A-wooing Go', which is embroidered in full colour on the Tea-time Tray.

Cross stitch is one of the easiest embroidery stitches to learn, and you do not have to be an expert to produce very acceptable results. Each project is accompanied with a charted design, a colour key and full step-by-step instructions for making it up.

Some of the designs are very easy to embroider and are quite suitable for beginners. Others are a little more challenging, with many colours and shaded effects, and will be of interest to craftspeople with a little more experience, or those who are keen to expand their scope.

There is also a Basic Skills section, which covers everything from preparing and stretching your fabric in an embroidery frame to mounting your cross stitching over card ready to be displayed.

Nothing has been left to chance – you will be able to cross stitch with confidence and enjoy making any of these projects to commemorate important events throughout the year, such as weddings, births, birthdays or the Christmas season.

$\mathcal{B}$ASIC SKILLS

■

BEFORE YOU BEGIN

PREPARING THE FABRIC

Even with an average amount of handling, many evenweave fabrics tend to fray at the edges, so it is a good idea to overcast the raw edges, using ordinary sewing thread, before you begin.

THE INSTRUCTIONS

Each project begins with a full list of the materials that you will require; Aida, Tula, Lugana and Linda are all fabrics produced by Zweigart. Note that the measurements given for the embroidery fabric include a minimum of 3cm (1¼in) all around to allow for stretching it in a frame and preparing the edges to prevent them from fraying.

A colour key for DMC stranded embroidery cotton is given with each chart. It is assumed that you will need to buy one skein of each colour mentioned, even though you may use less, but where two or more skeins are needed, this information is included in the main list of requirements.

Should you wish to use Coats/Anchor, or Madeira, stranded embroidery cottons, refer to the conversion chart given at the back of the book (page 48).

To work from the charts, particularly those where several symbols are used in close proximity, some readers may find it helpful to have the chart enlarged so that the squares and symbols can be seen more easily. Many photocopying services will do this for a minimum charge.

Before you begin to embroider, always mark the centre of the design with two lines of basting stitches, one vertical and one horizontal, running from edge to edge of the fabric, as indicated by the arrows on the charts.

As you stitch, use the centre lines given on the chart and the basting threads on your fabric as reference points for counting the squares and threads to position your design accurately.

WORKING IN A HOOP

A hoop is the most popular frame for use with small areas of embroidery. It consists of two rings, one fitted inside the other; the outer ring usually has an

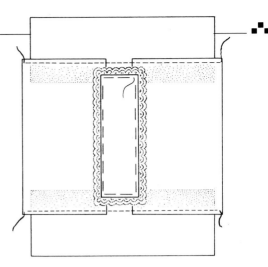

adjustable screw attachment so that it can be tightened to hold the stretched fabric in place. Hoops are available in several sizes, ranging from 10cm (4in) in diameter to quilting hoops with a diameter of 38cm (15in). Hoops with table stands or floor stands attached are also available.

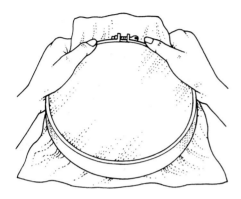

1 To stretch your fabric in a hoop, place the area to be embroidered over the inner ring and press the outer ring over it with the tension screw released. Tissue paper can be placed between the outer ring and the embroidery, so that the hoop does not mark the fabric. Lay the tissue paper over the fabric when you set it in the hoop, then tear away the central, embroidery area.

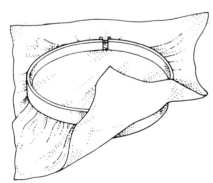

2 Smooth the fabric and, if needed, straighten the grain before tightening the screw. The fabric should be evenly stretched.

EXTENDING EMBROIDERY FABRIC

It is easy to extend a piece of embroidery fabric, such as a bookmark, to stretch it in a hoop.

● Fabric oddments of a similar weight can be used. Simply cut four pieces to size (in other words, to the measurement that will fit both the embroidery fabric and your hoop) and baste them to each side

of the embroidery fabric before stretching it in the hoop in the usual way.

WORKING IN A RECTANGULAR FRAME

Rectangular frames are more suitable for larger pieces of embroidery. They consist of two rollers, with tapes attached, and two flat side pieces, which slot into the rollers and are held in place by pegs or screw attachments. Available in different sizes, either alone or with adjustable table or floor stands, frames are measured by the length of the roller tape, and range in size from 30cm (12in) to 68cm (27in).

As alternatives to a slate frame, canvas stretchers and the backs of old picture frames can be used. Provided there is sufficient extra fabric around the finished size of the embroidery, the edges can be turned under and simply attached with drawing pins (thumb tacks) or staples.

1 To stretch your fabric in a rectangular frame, cut out the fabric, allowing at least an extra 5cm (2in) all around the finished size of the embroidery. Baste a single 12mm (½in) turning on the top and bottom edges and oversew strong tape, 2.5cm (1in) wide, to the other two sides. Mark the centre line both ways with basting stitches. Working from the centre outwards and using strong thread, oversew the top and bottom edges to the roller tapes. Fit the side pieces into the slots, and roll any extra fabric on one roller until the fabric is taut.

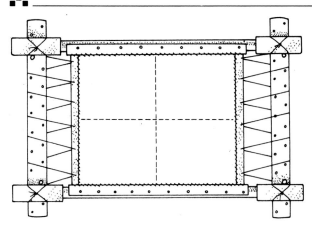

2 Insert the pegs or adjust the screw attachments to secure the frame. Thread a large-eyed needle (chenille needle) with strong thread or fine string and lace both edges, securing the ends around the intersections of the frame. Lace the webbing at 2.5cm (1in) intervals, stretching the fabric evenly.

ENLARGING A GRAPH PATTERN

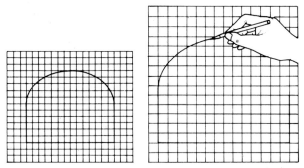

● To enlarge a graph pattern, you will need a sheet of graph paper ruled in 1cm (⅜in) squares, a ruler and pencil. If, for example, the scale is one square to 5cm (2in) you should first mark the appropriate lines to give a grid of the correct size. Copy the graph freehand from the small grid to the larger one, completing one square at a time. Use a ruler to draw the straight lines first, and then copy the freehand curves.

TO BIND AN EDGE

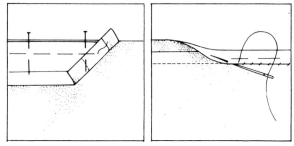

1 Open out the turning on one edge of the bias binding and pin in position on the right side of the fabric, matching the fold to the seamline. Fold over the cut end of the binding. Finish by overlapping the starting point by about 12mm (½in). Baste and machine stitch along the seamline.

2 Fold the binding over the raw edge to the wrong side, baste and, using matching sewing thread, neatly hem to finish.

PIPED SEAMS

Contrasting piping adds a special decorative finish to a seam and looks particularly attractive on items such as cushions and cosies.

You can cover piping cord with either bias-cut fabric of your choice or a bias binding; alternatively, ready-covered piping cord is available in several widths and many colours.

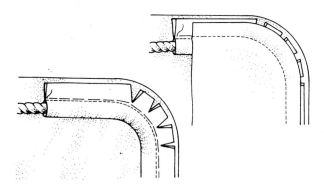

1 To apply piping, pin and baste it to the right side of the fabric, with seam lines matching. Clip into the seam allowance where necessary.

2 With right sides together, place the second piece of fabric on top, enclosing the piping. Baste and then either hand stitch in place or machine stitch, using a zipper foot. Stitch as close to the piping as possible, covering the first line of stitching.

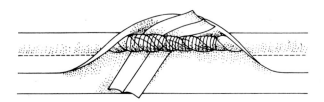

3 To join ends of piping cord together, first overlap the two ends by about 2.5cm (1in). Unpick the two cut ends of bias to reveal the cord. Join the bias strip as shown. Trim and press the seam open. Unravel and splice the two ends of the cord. Fold the bias strip over it, and finish basting around the edge.

MOUNTING EMBROIDERY

The cardboard should be cut to the size of the finished embroidery, with an extra 6mm (¼in) added all around to allow for the recess in the frame.

LIGHTWEIGHT FABRICS

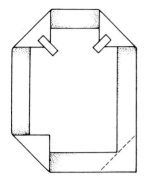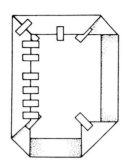

1 Place the emboidery face down, with the cardboard centred on top, and basting and pencil lines matching. Begin by folding over the fabric at each corner and securing it with masking tape.

2 Working first on one side and then the other, fold over the fabric on all sides and secure it firmly with pieces of masking tape, placed about 2.5cm (1in) apart. Also neaten the mitred corners with masking tape, pulling the fabric tightly to give a firm, smooth finish.

HEAVIER FABRICS

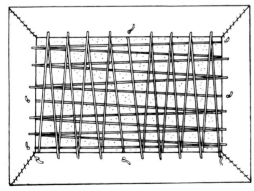

● Lay the embroidery face down, with the cardboard centred on top; fold over the edges of the fabric on opposite sides, making mitred folds at the corners, and lace across, using strong thread. Repeat on the other two sides. Finally, pull up the stitches fairly tightly to stretch the fabric firmly over the cardboard. Overstitch the mitred corners.

CROSS STITCH

For all cross stitch embroidery, the following two methods of working are used. In each case, neat rows of vertical stitches are produced on the back of the fabric.

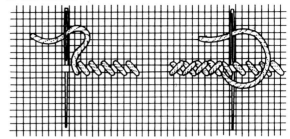

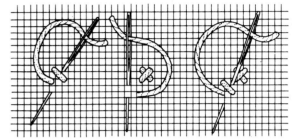

● When stitching large areas, work in horizontal rows. Working from right to left, complete the first row of evenly spaced diagonal stitches over the number of threads specified in the project instructions. Then, working from left to right, repeat the process. Continue in this way, making sure each stitch crosses in the same direction.

● When stitching diagonal lines, work downwards, completing each stitch before moving to the next.

BACKSTITCH

Backstitch is used in the projects to give emphasis to a particular foldline, an outline or a shadow. The stitches are worked over the same number of threads as the cross stitch, forming continuous straight or diagonal lines.

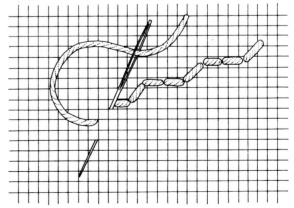

● Make the first stitch from left to right; pass the needle behind the fabric, and bring it out one stitch length ahead to the left. Repeat and continue in this way along the line.

Celebration Cushions

A pretty cushion, embroidered to celebrate a particular occasion, always makes a very acceptable gift. Each motif – confetti-strewn wedding bells, a floral Valentine heart and a Christmas wreath of poinsettias and holly – is bordered with ribbon, bows or braid, and each cushion is finished with delicate lace trim.

CELEBRATION CUSHIONS

YOU WILL NEED

For the Wedding Anniversary cushion, measuring overall 25cm (10in) square:

Two 25cm (10in) squares of white Davosa, 18 threads to 2.5cm (1in)
DMC stranded embroidery cotton in the colours given in the appropriate panel
140cm (1½yd) of white lace trim, 2.5cm (1in) wide
Gold embroidery thread for the border
23cm (9in) square cushion pad
No26 tapestry needle
Matching sewing thread

For the Christmas Time cushion, measuring overall 25cm (10in) square:

Two 25cm (10in) squares of khaki Aida, 16 threads to 2.5cm (1in)
DMC stranded embroidery cotton in the colours given in the appropriate panel
140cm (1½yd) of deep cream lace trim, 2cm (¾in) wide
23cm (9in) square cushion pad
No24 tapestry needle
Matching sewing thread

For the Valentine cushion, measuring overall 25cm (10in) square:

Two 23cm (9in) squares of white linen, 21 threads to 2.5cm (1in)
DMC stranded embroidery cotton in the colours given in the appropriate panel
140cm (1½yd) of white lace trim, 4cm (1½in) wide
180cm (2yd) of pink parcel ribbon
20cm (8in) square cushion pad
No26 tapestry needle
Matching sewing thread

WEDDING ANNIVERSARY

Baste the centre both ways on one of the squares of fabric and stretch it in a hoop, see page 4. Following the chart and colour key, and using two strands of thread in the needle throughout, begin the embroidery, stitching the gold thread details first. On this particular fabric, it is better to work one complete cross stitch at a time, over each intersection, to prevent the threads from slipping. Finish the embroidery and then outline the base of the bells in silver thread. Steam press on the wrong side.

For the border, follow the chart and, using two strands of gold thread in the needle, embroider the double lines, stitching under one thread and over five. Make sure that the pattern of stitching is the same on each line.

MAKING UP THE CUSHION

Trim the embroidery to measure 21.5cm (8½in) square. Using a tiny french seam, join the short edges of the lace together.

Run a gathering thread close to the straight edge of the lace. Pulling up the gathers to fit, lay the lace on the right side of the embroidery, with the decorative edge facing inwards and the straight edge parallel to the edge of the fabric and just inside the seam allowance. Baste in position, adjusting the gathers to allow extra fullness at the corners. Machine stitch in place.

With the right sides together, centre the backing fabric over the embroidered fabric and lace. Trim to size, then baste and machine stitch around, leaving a 13cm (5in) opening in the middle of one side. Remove all basting stitches; trim across the seam allowance at the corners, and turn the cover right side out. Insert the cushion pad and slipstitch the opening to close it.

CHRISTMAS TIME

Following the appropriate chart, complete the embroidery as for the Wedding Anniversary cushion. In this case, however, the design is embroidered on Aida fabric, so the cross stitches can be made in two stages, if you prefer. Embroider the backstitch details last of all.

Steam press the embroidery on the wrong side.

Trim the embroidery and backing fabric 24cm (9½in) square. Add the lace edging and make up the cushion following the previous instructions.

VALENTINE

Stretch the prepared fabric in a hoop and, following the relevant chart, complete the embroidery, using two strands of thread in the needle and working one cross stitch over two threads throughout. Steam press the finished embroidery on the wrong side.

For the ribbon border, cut the parcel ribbon into four 27.5cm (11in) lengths and four 17.5cm (7in) lengths. Withdraw a single thread from the ground fabric on each side, six threads out from the embroidered motif.

Following the diagram, thread one short length of ribbon from a point where two drawn-thread lines intersect and out to the nearest edge; take the ribbon under four threads and over six, leaving a tail for tying at the intersection.

Thread a longer length from the opposite edge of the fabric to meet the first at the same intersection, again leaving a tying thread at this point. Repeat on all sides to complete the ribbon border. The bows are tied after the cushion seams have been stitched, securing the outer ends of the ribbons.

FINISHING THE CUSHION

Trim the embroidery and the backing fabric to measure 20cm (8in) square. Add the lace edging and complete the cushion, following the instructions for the Wedding Anniversary cushion.

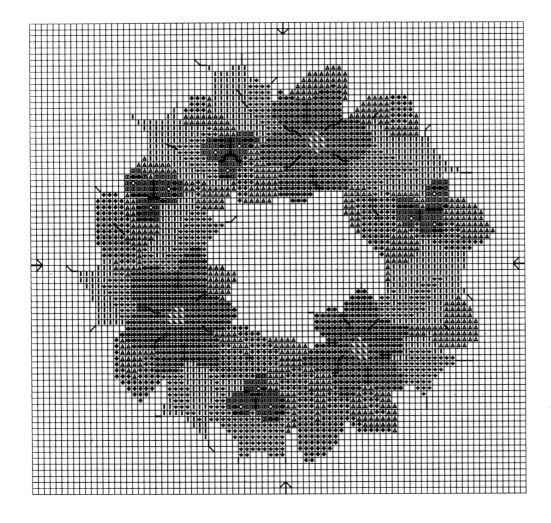

CHRISTMAS TIME ◄

◣ 725 yellow
○ 604 pink
⊡ 600 deep pink
✳ 606 red
● 915 purple (and bks poinsettia)
◆ 772 pale yellow green
△ 907 yellow green
I 955 pale green (bks 912)
↓ 912 veridian green

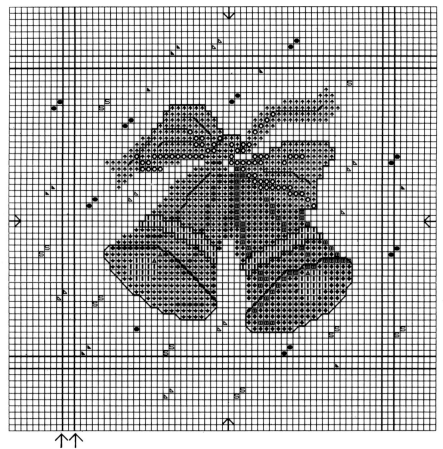

Stitching lines for the gold embroidery thread.

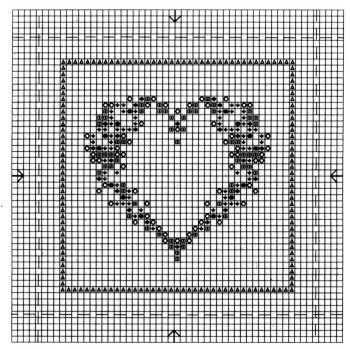

VALENTINE ▶

↓ 962 pink
● 601 red
○ 704 bright green
△ 733 olive green
⊡ 732 dark olive green
✱ 520 dark green

— — — Withdrawn thread line for ribbons.

Lacy Lavender Sachets

Sweet-scented lavender sachets are a traditional idea that will surely never go out of fashion.

These have been designed to be placed in a drawer, but if you wish to make them for use in hanging cupboards (perhaps to accompany a gift of padded coat hangers), you will need to purchase a slightly longer length of ribbon than the amount specified.

Although they are always called lavender sachets, remember that they can be filled with any type of potpourri. A summer garden mixture with rose petals would be particularly appropriate for the roses and violets design, for example. Alternatively, the strong, lemony scent of southernwood (*Artemisia abrotanum*) is a traditional defence against moths.

LACY LAVENDER SACHETS

YOU WILL NEED

For one sachet, with an overall measurement of 23cm × 15cm (9in × 6in):

50cm × 20cm (20in × 8in) of white openweave fabric, such as cotton Davosa or natural linen, 18 threads to 2.5cm (1in)
32.5cm (13in) of pre-gathered white lace trim, 4cm (1½in) wide
70cm (28in) of double-sided white satin ribbon, 1cm (⅜in) wide
DMC stranded embroidery cotton in the colours given in the appropriate panel
No26 tapestry needle
Matching sewing thread
Sufficient lavender or pot pourri to fill the sachet halfway

•

THE EMBROIDERY

To transfer the positioning lines to the embroidery, fold the fabric widthways in half and mark this line with a pin. Measure 8cm (3in) in from this point and baste across. Baste the upright centre line.

With the fabric held in a hoop, follow the chart and complete the motif, using two strands of thread in the needle. Where several colours are required, and to save time in starting and finishing, you may prefer to keep two or three needles in use, pinning them to the side when those particular colours are not being used.

Remove the basting stitches and steam press the finished embroidery on the wrong side.

MAKING UP THE SACHET

With the wrong side facing out, fold the fabric widthways in half; baste and machine stitch the sides, taking a 2.5cm (1in) seam. If the edges have frayed, check that the width of the sachet is 15cm (6in). Trim the seam allowances to 12mm (½in), and turn to the right side. Make a 4cm (1½in) single turning on the top edge and baste.

Join the short edges of the lace trim, using a tiny french seam. Pin and baste the trim to the inside of the top edge and, working from the right side, machine stitch in place, sewing close to the top edge.

Half fill the sachet with lavender and tie the ribbon twice around the top, finishing with the bow in front.

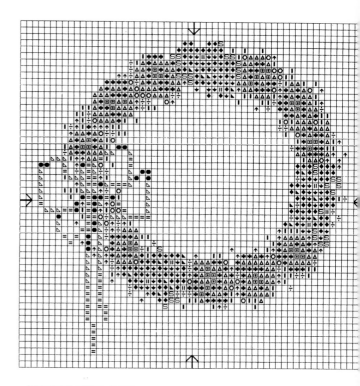

THE ROSE IS RED ▲

‖	445 yellow	✦	792 violet
△	3733 pink	=	3761 turquoise
✱	603 magenta	÷	959 veridian green
⊡	817 dark red	S	943 dark green
◆	341 pale blue	I	989 green
◺	794 blue	↑	471 olive
●	798 deep blue	○	3051 dark olive
◣	3609 mauve		

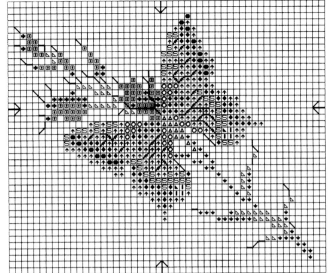

BUTTERFLY, BUTTERFLY ▲

↑ 445 yellow	◁ 989 green
◣ 783 ochre	↓ 993 veridian green
I 721 orange	○ 930 dark green blue
◆ 734 khaki (bks wing)	⊆ 340 light blue
⊡ 602 pink	● 792 dark blue
✱ 349 red	△ 824 navy blue

MARY, MARY ▲

- ‖ white (bks bloomers 930, collar 794)
- ◇ 745 pale lemon (bks butterfly wing 783)
- × 445 pale yellow
- ◁ 444 bright yellow
- ◆ 783 deep yellow
- ↑ 948 flesh (bks cockle shells 783)
- ⊡ 605 pink
- ● 603 deep pink
- ✱ 3705 red
- = 3761 pale blue
- ⊖ 3766 turquoise
- ↓ 930 slate grey (bks butterfly body)
- I 794 blue
- ⊆ 564 pale green
- △ 958 veridian green
- ÷ 3348 green
- ◣ 702 dark green
- ○ 3053 khaki

LAVENDER BLUE ▶

✱ 224 pink	△ 341 blue
● 892 geranium	↓ 368 green
⊡ 340 violet	(bks stems)

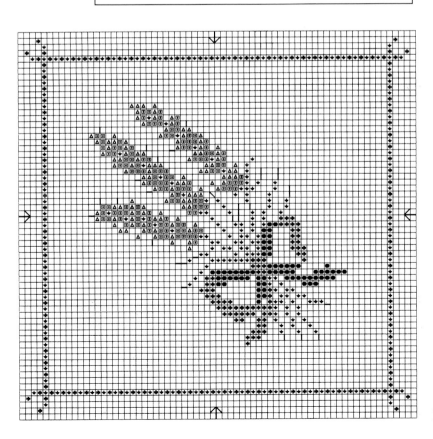

Tea-Time Tray

When guests call for tea, enchant them with this delightful tray, with its beautifully embroidered picture, safely protected under a glass surface. The theme – Anthony Rowley, the cheerful young frog, bearing an impressive bunch of flowers and about to call on Miss Mouse – would make this an amusing gift to bring to an engagement party. Instead of a tray, you might use it for the cover of a wedding-photo album.

A FROG HE WOULD A-WOOING GO ▲

6 white	▬ 3325 pale blue	△ 830 drab brown
L 727 yellow	I 312 dark blue	↓ 613 stone (and bks 611*)
◇ gold thread	A 734 light olive	T 415 pale grey
÷ 676 gold	(and bks 730*)	= 414 steel grey (bks 310)
◺ 680 deep gold	‖ 523 green	◣ 317 dark grey
⊢ 754 pale pink	◆ 367 dark green	● 310 black (bks 317)
(bks 352)	↑ 520 dark drab green	*Note: 2 additional*
⊡ 758 pink	◿ 435 light brown	*backstitch colours*
✱ 355 red	○ 832 golden brown	

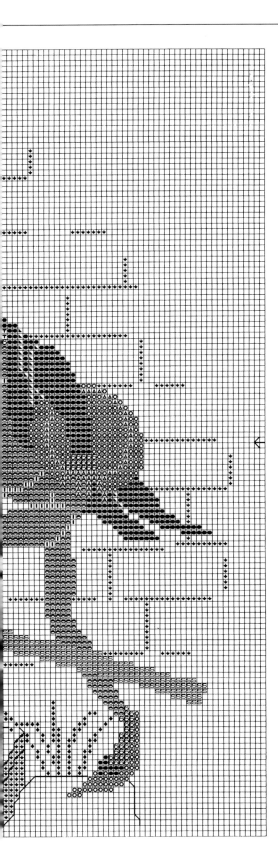

TEA-TIME TRAY

YOU WILL NEED

For a tray measuring 24cm (9½in) square:

*30cm (12in) square of cream evenweave
Hardanger, 18 threads to 2.5cm (1in)
DMC stranded embroidery cotton in the colours
given in the panel
No26 tapestry needle
Masking tape or strong thread for securing the
mounted fabric
Square wooden tray (for suppliers, see page 2)*

•

THE EMBROIDERY

With the prepared fabric stretched in an embroidery frame, see page 5, begin the cross stitching, using two strands of thread in the needle. Embroider the main characters first and then the background.

Finish by adding the backstitch details, using a single strand of thread.

Remove the design from the frame and steam press on the wrong side, if necessary.

ASSEMBLING THE TRAY

Using a soft pencil, mark the supplied mounting card both ways along the centre. This will help you to position the card exactly in the middle of the embroidery. Place the embroidery face down with the card on top and with the pencil lines and basting stitches matching.

Working on one side and then the opposite side, fold over the edges of the fabric on all sides, and secure with one or two pieces of masking tape. When you are sure the design is centred (if not, simply release the masking tape and adjust the fabric until it is correctly positioned), secure the corners firmly.

Turn in each corner to form a mitre (see page 7), and secure with masking tape. Next, finish securing the sides, stretching the fabric evenly, and finally, overcast the mitred corners to finish. Insert the mounted embroidery into the tray, following the manufacturer's instructions.

Christmas Tree Toys

Easily made from oddments of evenweave fabric, these brightly coloured tree toys, with their cross-stitched motifs stretched over cardboard shapes and with gold cord ties, take very little time to make. You can repeat the same motifs, or add your own designs, until you have sufficient toys to fill your Christmas tree. Alternatively, you might prefer to make a small selection each year, and in that way gradually build up your collection.

CHRISTMAS TREE TOYS

YOU WILL NEED

For the Candle and Bell, each measuring
9cm (3½in) across:

*Two 13cm (5in) squares of evenweave fabric,
14 threads to 2.5cm (1in), one in pale green
(candle) and one in pale blue (bell)
DMC stranded embroidery cotton in the colours
given in the appropriate panels
Two circles, 9cm (3½in) in diameter, of
3mm (⅛in) cardboard and two of lightweight
synthetic batting, cut to the same size
114cm (1¼yd) of gold cord, 3mm (⅛in) thick
No24 tapestry needle
Matching sewing thread*

For the Christmas tree and Santa Claus,
each measuring approximately 11cm × 10cm
(4½in × 4in):

*Two 18cm × 15cm (7¼in × 6in) rectangles of
evenweave fabric, 14 threads to 2.5cm (1in), one in
pale yellow (Santa Claus) and one in red
(Christmas tree)
DMC stranded embroidery cotton in the colours
given in the appropriate panels
Two 13cm × 10cm (5in × 4in) rectangles of
3mm (⅛in) cardboard, and two of lightweight
synthetic batting, cut to the same size
140cm (1½yd) of gold cord, 3mm (⅛in) thick
No24 tapestry needle
Matching sewing thread*

THE EMBROIDERY

All four of these Christmas tree hanging decorations
are embroidered and made up in the same way:
stretch the prepared fabric in a small hoop, see
page 4, and following the appropriate chart and
colour key, complete the embroidery, using two
strands of thread in the needle throughout. When
you have finished, press the embroidery on the
wrong side, retaining the basting stitches that mark
the centre lines.

MAKING UP THE TOYS

Following the chart, draw the outline of the appropriate toy on the cardboard, marking the arrows, and
cut out. Place the card shape on the batting, aligning
the arrows; draw around it with a pencil, and cut it
out. Mark the centre both ways on one side of the
cardboard – you can place it on the outline given
with the chart and pencil-mark the edge.

Lay the embroidery face down; centre the card
on top, with basting and pencil lines matching, and
lightly draw around. Draw a second line 12mm
(½in) outside and trim to this line. Cut the backing
fabric to this shape.

Lay the embroidery face down, centring the
batting and cardboard on top. Neatly fold over the
edges and hold them with adhesive tape. Remove

CHRISTMAS	✱ 602 magenta
TREE ▼	⊡ 3753 pale blue
◆ 677 pale	△ 911 green
yellow	(and bks tree)
(bks 606*)	*Note: one*
○ 972 yellow	*additional bks*
↓ 976 ochre	*colour**

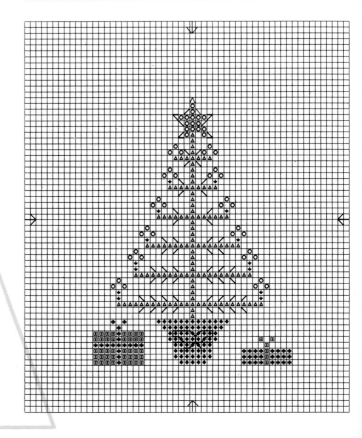

the basting threads, then turn in the edges of the backing fabric and pin them to the back. Using matching sewing thread, slipstitch around the edge.

Cut the cord into two equal lengths. Fold one length in half to find the central point and pin this to the centre of the bottom edge of the toy. Pin the cord around the toy, leaving the two long ends at the centre top for tying to the tree. Slipstitch around, firmly oversewing the join at the centre top of the toy.

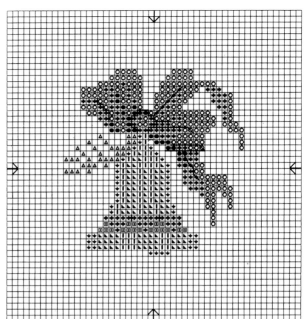

BELL ▶

▲	3078	lemon yellow	✽	224 dusky pink
I	743	yellow	●	961 deep pink
✦	972	deep yellow	⊡	799 blue
○	605	pink (bks 961)	△	911 green

CANDLE ▼

⊑	712	cream (and bks 928)	●	606 red
▲	743	pale yellow (bks 972)	✽	602 magenta
			△	958 veridian green (bks veins 911)
○	972	yellow	✦	911 green
◆	605	pink	⊡	928 grey

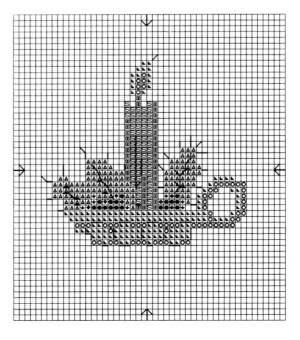

SANTA CLAUS ▲

▲	white		✽	606 red
◆	948	flesh		(bks 3799)
○	961	pink	△	799 blue
			●	3799 black

Christmas Greetings Cards

What better way to personalize your Christmas greetings than to embroider them yourself? Using prepared mounts, you can give them a truly professional finish. Once Christmas is over, the card mounts can be framed, so perhaps you might give a suitable frame as an accompanying gift. Three traditional Christmas rhymes – 'Little Jack Horner', 'Dame get up and bake your pies', and 'I saw three ships come sailing by' – have been used, but only the dame, with her Christmas decorations up, presents a very clearly Christmassy image. Either the three ships, or even Jack Horner, could be used for a birthday card, and the former would make a lovely parting gift for friends or family going to live abroad.

CHRISTMAS GREETINGS CARDS

YOU WILL NEED

For the *Little Jack Horner* card, measuring overall 20cm × 14.5cm (8in × 5¾in), with rectangular portrait cut out, 14cm × 9.5cm (5½in × 3¾in):

23cm × 18cm (9in × 7¼in) of blue evenweave
fabric (Aida), 18 threads to 2.5cm (1in)
DMC stranded embroidery cotton in the colours
given in the appropriate panel
No26 tapestry needle
Card mount (for suppliers, see page 2)

For the *Dame Get Up* card, measuring overall 20cm × 14cm (8in × 5½in) with oval portrait cut out, 14cm × 9.5cm (5½in × 3¾in):

23cm × 18cm (9in × 7¼in) of white evenweave
cotton (Linda), 27 threads to 2.5cm (1in)
DMC stranded embroidery cotton in the colours
given in the appropriate panel
No26 tapestry needle
Card mount (for suppliers, see page 2)

For the *I Saw Three Ships* card, measuring overall 20cm × 14.5cm (8in × 5¾in) with rectangular landscape cut out, 14cm × 9.5cm
(5½in × 3¾in):

23cm × 18cm (9in × 7¼in) of white (natural)
linen, 26 threads to 2.5cm (1in)
DMC stranded embroidery cotton in the colours
given in the appropriate panel
No26 tapestry needle
Card mount (for suppliers, see page 2)

●

THE EMBROIDERY

Prepare the fabric for each individual card in the same way and stretch it in a hoop, see page 4.

Bear in mind that very openweave linens tend to fray, so it is a good idea to overcast the edges beforehand.

Complete the cross stitching, using two strands of thread in the needle throughout. Finish by adding the backstitch details, using a single strand of thread. Remove the embroidery from the frame; take out the basting stitches, and steam press on the wrong side.

ASSEMBLING THE CARDS

Open out the self-adhesive card mount; centre your embroidered design over the window; trim to size, and fold over the left-hand side section. Press to secure.

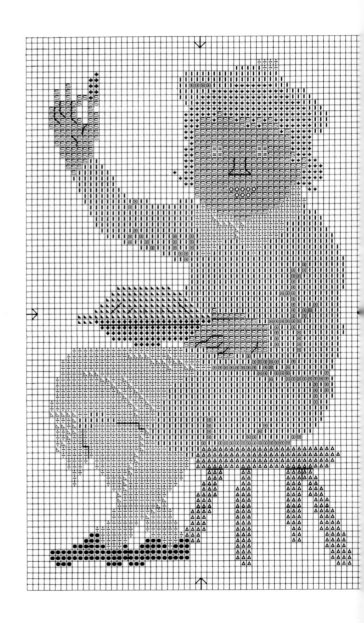

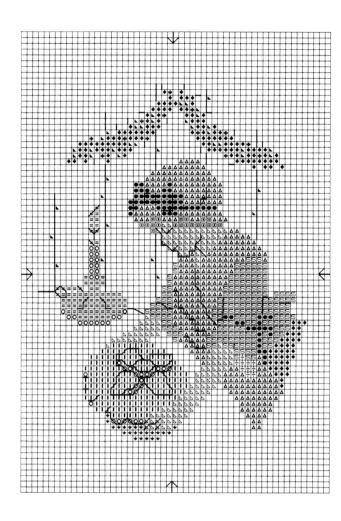

DAME GET UP ◀

÷ white
= 445 yellow (bks 833)
I 3047 gold (bks 833)
○ 833 deep gold
◺ 754 flesh (bks 605)
△ 605 pink (bks 335)
● 335 deep pink
✱ 350 red
◣ 800 pale blue (bks on wallpaper)
⊃ 3053 sage green (bks 992)
◆ 992 green
↓ 826 mid-blue (bks table top)
⊡ 611 brown

I SAW THREE SHIPS ▼

◣ 445 pale yellow   rigging on red
○ 726 yellow   and blue ships)
⊡ 833 ochre   ↓ 992 veridian green
● 350 red   (bks rigging on
△ 932 blue   green ship)
✱ 793 cornflower   I 471 green
    blue (bks

LITTLE JACK HORNER ◀

÷ white
△ 436 ochre (bks 435)
⊃ 948 flesh (bks 352)
○ 352 pink
✱ 550 purple
= 800 blue
I 368 green
⊡ 319 dark green
◣ 738 light brown (and bks 433*)
↓ 435 brown
◺ 415 grey
◆ 648 grey (bks 436)
● 310 black
*Note: one additional
backstitch colour**

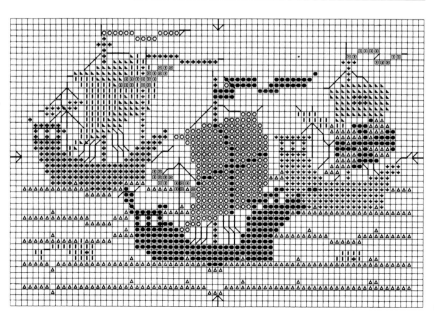

31

Traditional Sampler

The enduring appeal of the sampler –
worked here in the traditional style,
with borders and motifs in a single
colour – will ensure that this
delightful picture of the twelve
princesses becomes a favourite gift
for family and friends.
The sampler is designed to be
mounted in a frame, but if you choose
to embroider this design as a tray
cloth or table runner you
could easily increase the size
by setting the pairs of princesses
further away from the central
image of the magical night-time
castle, with its mysterious lake.

DANCING PRINCESSES ▲

3047 cream (bks on castle walls)   ● 349 red (and bks details)

TRADITIONAL SAMPLER

YOU WILL NEED

For a sampler measuring 24cm × 29cm
(9½in × 11½in):

*35cm × 40cm (14in × 16in) of pale khaki
evenweave Aida fabric, or linen,
16 threads to 2.5cm (1in)
DMC stranded emboidery cotton in the colour given
in the panel, plus 3 skeins of red 349, used for
the main colour
No24 tapestry needle
24cm × 29cm (9½in × 11½in) of lightweight
synthetic batting
24cm × 29cm (9½in × 11½in) of
medium-weight mounting board
Spray glue
Picture frame of your choice*

•

THE EMBROIDERY

With the prepared fabric stretched in a frame, see
page 5, and the centre lines basted both ways,
begin the embroidery. Using two strands of thread
in the needle, and carefully following the chart,
complete the cross stitching.

Remove the finished embroidery from the
frame; take out the basting stitches, and steam
press the work on the wrong side.

FRAMING THE SAMPLER

For a slightly padded effect, a thin layer of batting
is placed between the embroidery and the mounting board. Cut the batting to the same size as the
mounting board and attach it to the board with
spray glue or fabric adhesive. Mount the embroidery, following the instructions given for
heavier fabrics on page 7.

Insert the glass and the mounted embroidery
into your picture frame; add the backing board
provided, and tack in place. Cover the tacks with
broad sticky tape to neaten, and your sampler is
ready to hang up.

Victorian Mounts

Capturing the Victorian style of decorated picture mounts, these can be used to give a traditional effect to whatever you may wish to frame. The right-hand frame incorporates pearl beads in the shoe buckles and the elves' eyes, and the roses of the left-hand frame are similarly decorated. If you wish to set these behind glass, you could substitute stitches in a darker shade on the first, and omit beads from the roses.

VICTORIAN MOUNTS

YOU WILL NEED

For one picture mount with an overall measurement of 24cm × 19cm (9½in × 7½in); this includes 6mm (¼in) all around, for fitting into the recess of a picture frame:

30cm × 25cm (12in × 10in) of cream linen, 26 threads to 2.5cm (1in)
DMC stranded embroidery cotton in the colours given in the appropriate panel
24cm × 19cm (9½in × 7½in) of lightweight synthetic batting
30cm × 25cm (12in × 10in) of lightweight iron-on interfacing
24cm × 19cm (9½ × 7½in) of thin mounting card
Craft knife or sharp general purpose scissors
No26 tapestry needle and No9 crewel needle
Matching sewing threads
Tracing paper
Spray glue
All-purpose clear glue
Picture frame of your choice with a window area measuring 23cm × 18cm (9in × 7in)

•

THE EMBROIDERY

All three mounts are made in the same way. Stretch the fabric in a rectangular frame (see page 5). Using two strands of embroidery thread in the needle, and referring to the appropriate chart, complete the cross stitching. Remove the work from the frame and press the interfacing to the wrong side of the fabric. Using the crewel needle and matching thread, add the beads and pearls to the Elves and the Shoemaker and to Snow White and Rose Red respectively. If necessary, gently steam press the finished embroidery on the right side.

COMPLETING THE MOUNT

Using a soft pencil (2B), begin by tracing both the inner and outer lines of the frame given with the chart. Turn over the tracing; centre it on the card,

and trace through. Carefully cut out the window area, using a craft knife.

Cut the batting to the same shape as the mount, using the latter as a template, and then attach it to the mount with spray glue.

Mount the fabric, following the instructions for heavier fabrics, see page 7. With the wrong side facing, cut horizontally and vertically, and then cut diagonally across the centre both ways, cutting through both layers and snipping right up to the corners and to within 6mm (¼in) of the window edge. You will find that one or two tiny spots of clear glue, placed at the corners of the card, will help to secure the cut threads of the fabric. Trim across the flaps to straighten them, leaving allowances 12mm (½in) deep. Working on opposite sides, fold the allowances to the back of the card and secure them firmly with masking tape.

Centre your chosen photograph or painting behind the mount, securing it with masking tape before inserting the mount into the picture frame.

STITCHING ON BEADS

● Using either a fine crewel needle, number 9 or 10, or a beading straw for very fine beads, and sewing thread or fine silk, bring out the needle and thread on a bead. Reinsert the needle through the same hole, then make a stitch the width of the bead (and in this case, the width of the cross stitch), and pull through, with the thread below the needle. Repeat, completing the design as instructed.

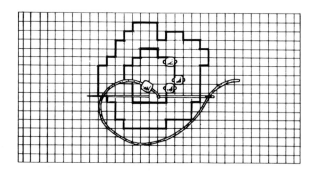

THE GOLDEN BIRD ▶

△ gold thread (bks 3052)
⊡ 3013 green (bks around tree and twigs)
✱ 3053 drab green
● 3052 dark drab green

ACKNOWLEDGEMENTS

The author would like to offer her grateful thanks to the following people who helped with the cross stitching of projects in this book with such skill and enthusiasm: Clarice Blakey, Caroline Davies, Christina Eustace, Janet Grey, Elizabeth Hall, Anne Whitbourn, and to Julie Hasler for her design on page 16.

The publishers would also like to thank The Monogrammed Linen Shop, 68 Walton Street, London SW3, and Thomas Goode and Co., 19 South Audley Street, London W1Y 6BN, for kindly supplying linen and china on page 16.
Thanks are also due to DMC Creative World Ltd for providing the black and white charts.

CONVERSION CHART

Not all of these colour conversions are exact matches, and bracketed numbers are given as close substitutes.

DMC	ANCHOR	COATS	MADEIRA	DMC	ANCHOR	COATS	MADEIRA	DMC	ANCHOR	COATS	MADEIRA
White	2	1001	White	676	891	2305	2208	899	(27)	3282	0505
224	893	3241	0813	677	(886)	2300	2207	907	255	—	1410
310	403	8403	Black	680	901	5374	2210	911	(205)	6205	1214
312	(147)	7979	1005	704	(256)	6238	1308	912	209	6225	1212
317	(400)	8512	1714	712	(387)	5387	2102	915	70	—	0705
319	(246)	6246	1313	721	(324)	2329	0308	924	(851)	6008	1706
335	(42)	3283	0506	722	(323)	2099	0307	927	(849)	6006	1708
340	118	7110	0902	725	(306)	2298	0108	928	(900)	7225	1709
341	117	—	0901	726	295	2294	0109	930	(922)	7052	1712
349	13	2335	0212	727	293	—	0110	943	188	—	1203
350	(11)	3011	0213	730	(924)	—	1614	948	(778)	2331	0306
352	(9)	3008	0303	732	(281)	—	1612	955	203	—	1210
355	5968	2339	0401	733	(280)	—	1611	958	187	6186	1114
367	(262)	6018	1312	734	(279)	—	1610	959	186	6185	1113
368	(261)	6016	1310	738	942	5375	2013	961	40	—	0610
414	(400)	8513	1801	743	(297)	2302	0113	962	52	—	0609
415	398	8510	1803	744	(301)	2293	0112	972	303	—	0107
433	(371)	5471	2008	745	(300)	2296	0111	976	(309)	—	2302
435	(365)	5371	2010	747	158	—	1104	989	(256)	6266	1401
436	(363)	5943	2011	754	(6)	2331	0305	992	(187)	6186	1202
444	291	2298	0108	758	868	2337	0403	993	(186)	—	1201
445	288	—	0103	761	(8)	3068	0404	3045	(888)	—	2103
451	—	—	1808	762	397	8510	1804	3047	(886)	2300	2205
452	—	—	1807	772	(264)	6250	1604	3051	(846)	—	1508
471	(280)	—	1501	783	307	—	2211	3052	(844)	—	1509
504	213	—	1701	792	941	7150	0905	3053	(859)	6315	1510
520	269	—	1514	793	121	721	0906	3072	847	—	1805
523	(215)	—	1512	794	120	—	0907	3078	292	2292	0102
550	(101)	4107	0714	798	(131)	7022	0911	3325	(159)	7976	1002
600	65	—	0704	799	(130)	7030	0910	3328	(11)	3071	0408
601	78	—	0703	800	(128)	—	0908	3347	(267)	6266	1408
603	(62)	3001	0701	817	47	2335	0211	3354	(75)	—	0608
605	(50)	3151	0613	824	(164)	—	1010	3609	(85)	—	0710
606	335	2334	0209	826	(161)	—	1012	3733	75	—	—
608	(333)	2332	0206	830	(906)	—	2114	3747	129	—	—
611	898	—	2107	832	907	—	2202	3753	(975)	—	—
613	831	—	2109	833	907	—	2114	3761	159	—	—
648	900	8390	1814	834	874	—	2204	3799	(152)	—	—